T0193690

Perfection Misconception

30 Devotionals For the Girl
Who Feels Less than Perfect

Karye Lynn McCord

WESTBOW
P R E S S®
A DIVISION OF THOMAS NELSON
& ZONDERVAN

WestBow Press books may be ordered through booksellers or by contacting:

WestBow Press
A Division of Thomas Nelson & Zondervan
1663 Liberty Drive
Bloomington, IN 47403
www.westbowpress.com
1 (866) 928-1240

Photograph taken by McKinley Jenkins.

Scripture taken from the King James Version of the Bible.

ISBN: 978-1-9736-6743-8 (sc)
ISBN: 978-1-9736-6742-1 (hc)
ISBN: 978-1-9736-6744-5 (e)

Library of Congress Control Number: 2019908735

Print information available on the last page.

WestBow Press rev. date: 9/13/2019

This book is dedicated to every girl who feels less than, you are not, you are enough.

ACKNOWLEDGMENTS

I would love to say a very big thank you to everyone who has helped me with this book. Thank you to Mrs. Misty Browning and Mrs. Marley Russell who looked over and helped me make sure my devotionals were biblically accurate. Thank you to my husband, Lynn McCord, who has stood beside me and supported me through everything, I love you. Last but not least, I want to say thank you to God for putting this on my heart and giving me ability and drive to complete my first devotional book.

CONTENTS

PREFACE

Perfection Misconception is a devotional book I have written for the girl who feels less than perfect. I hope this book helps you to realize that being perfect isn't about doing everything right, but it's about fearlessly following God and seeking after what he wants for your life. The misconception with being a Christian woman in this day and time is that we will never make mistakes because of our faith, and that is not the case, we are not spiritually, mentally, or physically perfect. We are humans and we do make mistakes and when we do all eyes are on us for messing up. It's scary to live courageously for God for the fear of condemnation by the world when we do fall short. BUT, you have to remember that our goal is not to make the world happy, but to make God happy. Along the way we are sure to fail, but because, again we are not perfect, we just have to keep on for Christ. Ask for forgiveness for our shortcomings and brush off the dirt and keep running! No, we are not perfect, but our God is! I hope this book helps to set you free from whatever is keeping you out of the race for God. I pray this book conveys God's love and compassion he has for his children. I pray this book helps you, the girl who falters, the girl who feels like she messes up everything. I hope you find little victories in your walk with Christ. This book comes from my heart, it has been a long time in the making as the devil has fought me at every turn. This is my calling. I am no singer, I cannot play a musical instrument, but I can write, and I hope these writings in this book bring glory to God and help to you, my sister in Christ.

TODAY'S TAKE AWAY
(write or doodle your thoughts for the day)

PROVERBS 31:25-31

Verse 30:
"Favour is deceitful, and beauty is vain: but a woman that feareth the Lord, she shall be praised."

If you even know a little bit about the Bible you know about the virtuous woman in Proverbs 31! This woman, though she is not named, is very important she teaches us what a woman should be! I know it's scary reading this and thinking, I can't do all of this I'm not perfect?!?! BUT, you can, see, just like me and you this woman is just a person. She's not a higher being or a sinless woman, but she does seek after God. This woman is no doubt very devoted to the things of God. He is obviously number one in her life, and it shows. To me, she is very intimidating because she seems perfect, and I know I could never measure up to perfection. In reality though, she is really just a sinner saved by grace following after God, and I feel almost certain that she made some mistakes along the way, but she asked for forgiveness and repented, just as we are able to! Then, I imagine she would learn from the mistakes that she made and move on! Even better than that, God forgave her! He forgives his children when we repent. This woman is a great example for that. The epitome of saved by Grace, so next time you feel overwhelmed or discouraged, or less than perfect think about the virtuous woman! She wasn't virtuous because she was perfect, but because she sought after God!

TODAY'S TAKE AWAY
(write or doodle your thoughts for the day)

JAMES 3:5-12

Verse 8:
"But the tongue can no man tame; it is an unruly evil, full of deadly poison."

In this verse unruly is being referred to as restless, in a sense that the tongue can not stop being evil. That is our fleshly nature, to talk about others and what we think they are doing wrong. Verse 10 tells us "Out of the same mouth proceedeth blessing and cursing. My brethren, these things ought not so to be." The next few verses in James 3 tells us water coming out of a fountain can't be sweet and bitter if it's coming from the same place. It also says that a fig tree can't grow olives. These are both examples of the fact that we as Christians can't sit and gossip about people and be okay with it, or we shouldn't be okay with it at least. I will be the first to tell you that for me it's hard to hold my tongue sometimes. Especially when I'm mad or I feel like I've been done wrong. It's just so easy, you're with your friends, no one is going to hear your conversation and you just go on and tell what you know, or what you heard, or your judgmental opinion on someone else's life. It's that easy, except it's not, especially when you belong to God. It will come back to bite you, I know from experience. That's still a thing I battle with gossip in my life because it's what I did for so long I talked about people, primarily if they made me angry or "did me wrong" and let me be the first to tell you the devil knows how to push the right buttons at the right time to try to get me to say something and more times than not I cave just a little whether my reaction is something as small as me turning up my nose or I actually say something negative about the person or their actions. That's something I have to pray daily about. It's one of my thorns, but it's gotten better. On days I succeed I know that it is purely from God. He gives us the strength we need to slay our sinfulness. In this chapter it talks about how the tongue is uncontrollable and evil, but with the Grace of God we are able to overcome these difficulties my bible had a great side note that I read "Remember that we are not fighting the tongues fire in our strength. The Holy Spirit will give us increasing power to monitor and control what we say."

3

TODAY'S TAKE AWAY
(write or doodle your thoughts for the day)

Verse 34
"And, behold, the whole city came out to meet Jesus:
and when they saw him, they besought him that he
would depart out of their coasts."

This is the story of when Jesus was passing through Gergesenes and
He finds the two men with demons. Jesus cast the demons out of the
men and into a herd of swine (pigs). Then, the swine ran into the
sea and died. After that, it goes on to tell that the swine keepers ran
back to to the city to tell everyone what happened, and the whole
city came out to meet Jesus. If you know much about the Bible you'll
realize this is where Jesus is going around doing miracles, and as
many times as I've heard this story I'd never realized what the last
verse of this story was saying. "And, behold, the whole city came
out to meet Jesus: and when they saw him, they besought him that
he would depart out of their coasts." Now, besought means begged,
that means that THEY LITERALLY BEGGED JESUS TO LEAVE!!
How bonkers is that?!? Two men just got demons cast out of them,
and the people of the city are so worried about the fact that they
lost the pigs. They didn't care about the miracles Jesus had just
performed! Sometimes, I think we are still like that we don't see the
miracles Jesus works for us everyday. If you notice the next verse
after 34, which is "And he entered into a ship, and passed over, and
came into his own city."(Matthew, verse 1, chapter 9, KJV) . Jesus
got back on a ship and passed over. If you want Jesus to leave He
will, He won't tarry where he is not wanted. If you get so wrapped
up in the things of this world that you forget or put Jesus in the back
seat. He will leave you alone. That is the scariest thought, is it not?
He is an all or nothing God. Not a Sunday, Wednesday, and any day
you get into some trouble God. He wants your whole life. He won't
share with the world.

TODAY'S TAKE AWAY
(write or doodle your thoughts for the day)

Verse 17:
"Pray without ceasing"

I love Chapter 5 of 1 Thes. it just gives me so much encouragement. Here lately I have been going through a slump. Lots of things have been going on in my life and it's really gotten me down. We all get like that sometimes, sad. It's okay to be sad, we have emotions and it's okay to express them. It's when sadness takes over your life, that's when the problems start. The devil will do anything to get you down and out especially to get you to stop praying or reading your bible. He knows your weaknesses and he's not afraid to use them, but we have to remember that we know someone who is more powerful than the devil, more powerful than the sadness! We have Jesus Christ, and for that we should rejoice! When life starts to take a turn for the worse often times we like to run away and sulk, I know i'm guilty of it. I'll get so low I don't even feel like I can pray, and the devil wants us to constantly stay in that state, but we can't! We must keep on and keep praying! Verse 17 says we must pray WITHOUT ceasing that means when things are going great and when things are going bad!! We as Christians often times forget that. Prayer is a direct hotline to God, why wouldn't we use it! So, next time you're feeling sad or down or even happy and thankful don't forget to pray!

TODAY'S TAKE AWAY
(write or doodle your your thoughts for the day)

Verse 21:
"This I recall to my mind, therefore have I hope"

Have you ever felt like you're just so weighed down by the things of this world? You just feel beaten down and as if you can't seem to even catch a breath without something else seemingly bad happening to you? That's how Jeremiah felt and he tells about it in this chapter. Jeremiah is writing to tell us about how much affliction he has in his life and how he is bound up and feels like he is the most miserable person. He tells about his sorrows and how he feels like God doesn't even hear his prayers. He goes on to tell that he feels desolate and that he feels that his strength is perished, but then we hit verse 21. Therefore have I hope those four words. He writes that even through the hardest times of our lives the Lord's mercies and his compassion fail us not! His faithfulness to us is great even when we are weak. We just have to seek him, even in the storms we need to seek God's will for our lives. Bro. Warren Wiersbe brought this thought to light, "When we go through the serious trials and storms of our lives we are quick to ask 'HOW can I get out of this' when we should be asking 'WHAT can I get out of this' we need seek to what God has for us through the storms". (Wiersbe, Warren)

TODAY'S TAKE AWAY
(write or doodle your thoughts for the day)

"Pilate saith unto them, What shall I do then with Jesus which is called Christ? They all say unto him, let him be crucified."

This verse is possibly one of the saddest in the whole Bible. Right here Pilate has brought forth Barabbas a criminal and Jesus the innocent and he asked the people who to set free and who to condemn. The people set Barabbas free. They condemned Jesus to die on the cross. The phrase that pounds in my head head when I read this verse is "What shall I do with Jesus?" What are you doing with Jesus? Are you living for Him, studying His word, praying or are you letting Barabbas free? Are you letting sin take over your life and hanging Jesus on the cross? Reading about Jesus being crucified always puts knots in my stomach, because I know He endured the pain and suffering for me and you. So why in the world would we not want to live our lives for Him? He was beaten as the crowd cheered. He endured it all for us. He cares for us, HE LOVES US! To put it into perspective think of the one person you love the most, the person that you would do anything for. You love that person so so so much, but would you be willing to die an excruciating death for them? Have the skin of your back ripped off, thorns smashed into your head, nails driven through your hands and feet? I'm not going to lie, I don't know if I could take all of that, but Jesus did. He took the beatings, the mockery, the thorns, the nails, all for you. Just to show you how much He truly loves you. So, What are you going to do with this man called Jesus?

TODAY'S TAKE AWAY
(write or doodle your thoughts for the day)

LUKE 6: 41-42

Verse 41:
"And why beholdest thou the mote that is in thy brother's eye, but perceivest not the beam that is in thine own eye?"

Do you ever find yourself people watching or scrolling through a social media platform and thinking "wow I can't believe they are doing that, and they call themselves Christians," because I have. So many times we find ourselves calling out other people's sins when we rarely take a step back and look at ours. We are so quick to pass judgment on others without even thinking of our own downfalls. What does that make us? A hypocrite. We act as if we are perfect and never do anything wrong, all while just hiding our sins a little better than someone else. If we really want to help anyone, first we have to evaluate ourselves. We have to repent of all our sins and we have to actively seek the word of God, and we have to learn not to judge others. We are not God.... nor should we pretend to be by judging others. I think we forget that fact a lot of times. We have faults and sins just like the people we are judging. We should show love and compassion to the people we see lost and astray not look down on them and judge them. We aren't called to do that, we are called to show love and compassion to them through the scriptures and to hold out a helping hand to those who stumble and fall. We should be there to pray them through their battles, not add insult to injury. When those people see compassion in us Christians it will help them to see God's love, and what He has planned for us!

Challenge: Next time you see a fellow Christian, or anyone, struggling instead of talking about them pray for them!

This will not only help them but, it will help you and your relationship with God too!

TODAY'S TAKE AWAY
(write or doodle your thoughts for the day)

MATTHEW 5:13

"Ye are the salt of the earth: but if the salt have lost his savour, where with shall it be salted? It is thenceforth good for nothing, but to be cast out, and to be trodden under the foot of man."

Matthew chapter five has a lot to teach us in itself, but verse 13 is the one I want to focus on today. Who doesn't love salt?! I know I do, it can add flavor and life to something that is bad or bland and make it good again! In verse 13 God tells us that WE are the salt of the Earth! God calls us to spread His word like we would spread salt on a meal! I know, often times I fail to tell people about God and what He has done for me, or I get scared and decide not to mention Him because I don't want to make someone uncomfortable or mad, but I shouldn't, WE shouldn't be that way!! WE ARE SALT! We should be spreading His word not keeping it to ourselves, what good is salt if you never use it? In the latter part of this verse God shows us that if the salt have lost his savor it's good for nothing, too many times in my walk with Christ I feel like I'm no good because some days it's hard to even pick up a Bible. How are we supposed to tell people about God if we won't even spend 15 minutes in His word. What do you do with salt that isn't any good any more? You throw it away or "cast out" the bad salt that's what the Bible says will happen to us if we lose our savor. I don't know about you, but I don't ever want to be cast out by God, I want Him to always use me, and my life as a living testimony of His mercy and grace. I want to be salt!

TODAY'S TAKE AWAY
(write or doodle your thoughts for the day)

Verse 9:
"The meek will he guide in judgment: and the meek will he teach his way."

Have you ever wondered why God wasn't using you? You feel like you have so many good qualities, but you just can't seem to find the right thing to do? Maybe it's because your ego is in the way. You can't be boastful and expect God to use you in the furtherance of His kingdom. He wants the meek. Nowadays, we think of meek as being weak, but it's not! Being a meek Christian means that you are willing to submit to God's will for your life. Meekness is one of the greatest qualities a Christian can have! So much so that it's in the Beatitudes in Matthew 5! We should want our lives to make God proud, not anyone else. So, if you are really trying to seek after God and his plans for your life, start by learning to be meek! Verse 9 doesn't say and the "stubborn" or the "proud" or the "boastful", but the meek will He teach His way!

TODAY'S TAKE AWAY
(write or doodle your thoughts for the day)

Verse 19:
"Wherefore, my beloved brethren, let every man be swift to hear, slow to speak, slow to wrath:"

I have such a quick temper. I get so angry so quickly and sometimes it's over the smallest things. I've really been trying lately to control my temper. These verses have really been on my mind, really the first couple of chapters of James. We are called to be doers of the word (James 1:22*) and getting angry hinders that. How are we supposed to let our light shine for others when the only thing they see in us is anger and bitterness? We have to lay down our flesh daily and realize that we must be submissive to God and His word. We can't just be hearers of God's word and expect to receive blessings from God we must be doers. We might be the only Jesus someone sees and what would they think if the only thing they seen in us was anger. When you begin to share God's love with others the devil will come after you full force using anything he can to trip you up. He knows all the right buttons to push to get you to fail, and sometimes you do fail. We all fall short of the Glory of God. But, the great thing is that God picks us right back up and gives us another chance to shine our light for Him. So, whatever you are struggling with whether it be anger or gossip or any other thing know that it is overcomeable, we just have to lay down our flesh and pick up our cross.

*** *"But be ye doers of the word, and not hearers only, deceiving your own selves." James 1:22***

TODAY'S TAKE AWAY
(write or doodle your thoughts for the day)

Verse 7:
"So when they continued asking him, he lift up himself, and said unto them, He that is without sin among you, let him first cast a stone at her."

The other day I was listening to one of my favorite songs "Sands of Time" by the Carr Family and while I have listened to this song tons of times it really hit me in a different way. This is a song about the woman that was accused of committing adultery. The Scribes and Pharisees brought her into the temple while Jesus was there. They wanted Him to condemn her for her sins, but instead of condemning her, Jesus told her accusers "...He that is without sin among you, let him first cast a stone at her." (John, verse 7, chapter 8 KJV). Jesus, instead of condemning her of her sins reminded all of those Scribes and Pharisees that we are not the judge of other people and their sins, just because they got caught in their sins doesn't mean that you couldn't just as easily be in that situation. I think we often times forget that we sin. We will see all the good things that we do as a person and think we have arrived, so much so that we will begin to think that we can tell others where they are wrong or when they have sinned. That is not the case, nor will it ever be the case we are not exempt from sin so we should never judge other people and the sins they are in. We are supposed to show compassion on all people no matter the sin we are to love and show them Jesus and leave the judging to God.

TODAY'S TAKE AWAY
(write or doodle your thoughts for the day)

"But let your Yea, yea; Nay, nay: for whatsoever is more than these cometh of evil."

This comes out of a passage called the Beatitudes. It describes how we as Christians are supposed to be/act. It's a great idea to read through those chapters a good bit because they really show what a Christians life should be like. As I read through them this morning verse 37 really caught my attention. It's talking about our communication with others. It says let your yea be yea and your nay be nay which basically means, say what you mean, and mean what you say. So many times I find myself guilty of making "empty promises" to someone, to myself, and even to God. It isn't always a big promise it may just be that I'll read my bible more, or that I won't spend as much time on my phone. Or, the ever so classic I'll get up earlier and work out. These may all be simple things but they were empty. Verse 37 tells us to mean what we say, whether we want to or not. If you say you are going to do it, do it. We are supposed to be people of our word, not just someone who might do what they say. God never turned back on anything He said He would do, so why should we?

TODAY'S TAKE AWAY
(write or doodle your thoughts for the day)

Verse 4:
"Are ye not then partial in yourselves, and are become judges of evil thoughts?"

We as people are so judgy. I am so judgy. Sometimes we see an easy opportunity to bring someone down and we take it, but we shouldn't be that way especially if we are Christians (or claim to be). It gets so easy to get into the flesh and treat someone better because they have more money or they have nicer house and that's not how things should be. We should treat everyone with the same honor and respect that we would want. So often we hear the phrase "Treat others how you want to be treated". That comes from "Therefore all things whatsoever ye would that men should do to you, do ye even so to them: for this is the law of the prophets." (Matthew, verse 12, chapter 7, KJV). Honestly, how often do we follow that? I know what you're thinking "Well I'm nice to everyone I meet." Are you really though? Have you ever smiled to someone's face but had an ugly thought about them? That's really what this means, we can't just outwardly be nice we have to inwardly be nice too! God does a work on our insides before He ever touches the outside. We are not put on this Earth to smile and silently judge people, we are put here to do and share God's word. Besides, what does that mean thought do for you other than boost your own ego. Nothing, it does nothing for you. So remember, be nice from the inside out.

TODAY'S TAKE AWAY
(write or doodle your thoughts for the day)

Verse 2
"Examine me, O Lord, and prove me; try my reins and my heart."

Do you ever use the phrase, "now, don't judge me" before you say you like or dislike something? Maybe a singer or a pair of shoes. I know I do all time. Honestly, who really wants to be judged anyways... most of the time we as people don't always think just alike, so our opinions are different. There is one person though, who has the best opinion and that is God! In these verses you find David asking God to judge him and examine his life so that he won't slide or stray away from what God wants for his life. Sometimes I think we forget that God is always watching us. He sees our true reactions when no one else would. He sees how quick to anger and judgment we are, and when I remember that fact, it always makes me remorseful because if another person seen me act that way they could question if I was a Christian or not. This is something I struggle with, asking God to show me what I need to work on, but it is something that has to be done or we will still have that besetting sin, and I don't want my arrogance or unwillingness to work on my sin keep someone else from seeing Christ.

So, I challenge you to really ask God to show you what sin you have holding you back and pray about it and work on controlling it, you never know who it might help.

TODAY'S TAKE AWAY
(write or doodle your thoughts for the day)

PROVERBS 10:4

"He that becometh poor that dealeth with the slack hand: but the hand of the diligent maketh rich."

On initial reading you think this verse is about making money. While it could apply that way I want to look at it from a spiritual perspective. Slack means lazy. So, when we are lazy with the Lord we become poor in spirit. I know if I go even a day without reading my bible or praying my days don't feel the same and I'm almost embarrassed the next time I try to pray, because God knows I was slack in and with His word. "...The hand of the diligent, though, becomes rich in spirit." (Proverbs, verse 4, chapter 10, KJV) That's not just opening your bible and reading two sentences and closing it and never thinking about it again for the rest of the day. Being diligent in study is really comprehending what you are reading and earnestly praying about the things/ people in your life. I'm by no means perfect, but I am so thankful I serve a God who is, and who loves me despite of my slack in the study of his word. We must be diligent in our study time with God, and we must share what we know not just keep it to ourselves. You may be the only Jesus someone ever sees and I wouldn't want to be caught slacking.

TODAY'S TAKE AWAY
(write or doodle your thoughts for the day)

1 TIMOTHY 4:8

"For bodily exercise profiteth little: but godliness is profitable unto all things, having promise of the life that now is, and of that which is to come."

We go to the gym to keep our physical bodies in shape, but are we going to the spiritual gym? We as humans are obsessed with physical health, we eat right, some even make daily trips to the gym, but do we ever think about keeping our faith in shape? We will take time our of our "busy day" to go to the gym and work out, but we don't have time to read our Bibles or we are too tired to go to Church. Our spiritual bodies have become couch potatoes. How are we supposed to run the race and fight a good fight if we only study God's word once or twice a week? We can't!!! Just like to keep our physical bodies in shape we have to constantly work at it to see progress! If we want to be knowledgeable and found faithful for the Lord we have to constantly study His word! So, let me ask you this; are you a member of Heaven's gym?

TODAY'S TAKE AWAY
(write or doodle your thoughts for the day)

PROVERBS 16:9

"A man's heart deviseth his way, but the Lord directeth his steps."

We all have plans and hopes and dreams for our lives, but have you ever found yourself somewhere and you have absolutely no idea how you ended up there? Sometimes we get carried away in trying to make our life what we want it to be and not what God wants it to be. We will get so caught up in ourselves that we forget to pray and ask God if this is His will and what He wants for us. We make plans for our future not asking if that's where the Lord wants us to be. That will get us into trouble, because you can say what your plan is all you want, but if it's not God's will it won't ever happen. God has our futures picked out for us and we need to pray for His will for our lives not our own, because we could miss out on our opportunity to serve Him if we are not where He wants us to be. I don't know about you, but at the throne it would break my heart a million times over to hear Him say 'if you would have just sought after my will and what I had planned for you.' We can't be scared of what we don't know, if it's God's plan then there is a way, and that's a fact Jack! If you feel the Lord is calling you to do something seek His will without fear of tomorrow because He is always there for His children!

TODAY'S TAKE AWAY
(write or doodle your thoughts for the day)

1 CORINTHIANS 16:14

"Let all your things be done in Charity."

Have you ever done anything nice for someone and expected something in return? Yeah, me too. It's human nature, I suppose, that we expect to get repaid. We shouldn't think like that though. In the Bible, Charity means love. We should do all things out of love. We shouldn't expect to be rewarded for being a "nice person". We can't walk around thinking that the world owes us something for being a good neighbor like the Bible tells us to be! We need to be kind and that's it. We can't expect for people to repay us, because then we would walk around with hurt feelings when we don't get back the same effort we put out. So, live your life out of love, be kind just to be kind. The rewards await us in Heaven.

TODAY'S TAKE AWAY
(write or doodle your thoughts for the day)

"As the hart panteth after the water brooks, so panteth my soul after thee, O God."

Have you ever wanted something so badly. So bad that you thought if you didn't get it you just might die without it. Bad enough that you would do almost anything to have it? Maybe that one job, the new car, that one perfect guy? We all have things that we think we need. We strive to get those things, we will do whatever it takes for us to try to reach our "dream goals". Now, let me ask this.... Do you strive that hard to have a relationship with God? Are you doing all you can to take time out of your day to pray or read your Bible? In this verse a "hart" is a deer and that deer has to have water to survive. It is panting after the water, this deer is showing us the way we should be seeking after God! He should be the most important thing in our lives. After all, He is the LIVING water.

TODAY'S TAKE AWAY
(write or doodle your thoughts for the day)

LAMENTATIONS 3:40

"Let us search and try our ways, and turn again to the Lord."

Lamentations is a book written by Jeremiah. It's actually the lamentations of Jeremiah, and Lamentations means: the passionate expression of grief or sorrow; weeping. So these are actually the accounts of Jeremiah's grief and sorrow. Chapter 3 starts out by saying how Jeremiah would rather be dead he has so much pain and is under so much torture by life, but in verse 20 his tone changes and he talks about the Lord's mercy and faithfulness to him. I've read this story countless times, but this time verse 40 caught my eye. It's Jeremiah telling about searching and trying his own ways, but turning again to the Lord. After verse 40 he continues to tell about how the Lord is faithful even though we have transgressed and rebelled He still forgives us. Reading that one verse brought back countless memories of times in my life where I thought I knew a better way than the way God had laid out for me. Lots of times in our lives we feel like we know better than God. We think that our way is best. Maybe it's in a career, or a friendship, or even a relationship. I know I would have been in a lot less pain if I wouldn't have tried to take my dating life into my own hands. We are so quick to think that we know best when all we can see is the here and now, we don't know what two days in the future holds much less 10 years. So many things could change so why not trust that our future is safe in God's hands, and just leave the "our way" out of it.

TODAY'S TAKE AWAY
(write or doodle your thoughts for the day)

Verse 31:
"But they that wait upon the Lord shall renew their strength; they shall mount up with wings as eagles; they shall run, and not be weary; and they shall walk, and not faint."

Have you ever felt so overburdened and worried that you just don't think you can go on? I think we all have.... We get to that point when we just absolutely can not bear it on our own, but great news! We don't have to! We may be weary and ready to give up, but our God is NOT! He is never weary, but everlasting!! He will give you the the strength you need. As worldly people we will surely fail and lose strength, but when our hope and faith is in God He will renew our strength. We won't grow weary or faint. We just have to have faith that God will deliver us from whatever we are going through. Whether that be taking us out of the storm, or giving us peace IN the middle of the storm!

TODAY'S TAKE AWAY
(write or doodle your thoughts for the day)

PSALMS 20

Verse 7:
"Some trust in chariots, and some in horses: but we will remember the name of the Lord our God."

Do you ever find yourself relying more on the things of this world than God? Too often, we put our faith in material things or people rather than the one who created it all. We think that we can always rely on the world to make things happen. We are even bad to rely on ourselves for things, we think that we are good enough to get ourselves by, and that is not the case. If it were up to the world, or me or you we would all be lost, headed to hell. Nothing we could ever do would change that. We are nothing but wicked creatures, but God, He has a plan for us. He is the one that we can depend on! People and things will fail you miserably, but our Lord will give you joy and peace beyond belief. He will never fail you!

TODAY'S TAKE AWAY
(write or doodle your thoughts for the day)

PHILIPPIANS 1:12

"But I would ye should understand, brethren that the things which happened unto me have fallen out rather unto the furtherance of the Gospel;"

Sometimes things in life don't go as planned. We never expect the bad things to happen to us, but they do and when that happens sometimes it's really hard to see what good could possibly come from such tragedy. We always want to ask God "why did that have to happen that way? Why did they have to die? Why did they break up with me?" We don't always understand. I know the saying 'Everything happens for a reason' is a little redundant, but it is so very relevant. Sometimes I think we forget that God is in control and that He knows what we need more than we know. God's timing for everything in our lives is perfect and that's why we should find the silver lining in the bad situations that are thrown at us. Everything that happens to us in our Christian walk is to bring honor and glory to God. We must praise Him for everything in our lives, the good and the bad. Maybe God is putting you through a trial right now so that when you come out on the other side you're able to show people that are going through the same battle that they are not alone and you're able to witness to them that way. That is furtherance of the Gospel my friend. So, just remember that even in the hard times we are to keep the faith and share the Gospel and what God has done for you in your life.

TODAY'S TAKE AWAY
(write or doodle your thoughts for the day)

1 PETER 4:8-9

"Use hospitality one to another without grudging."

It's easy to have love for people when everything in your life is going good and it seems like you've got it all figured out. What about when things aren't going your way and great things keep happening to everyone but you? It's a little harder then. I know it is for me, anyways, but we see good things happening to those around us and we can't seem to catch a break. We begin to get sad, jealous, or even angry. That's not the way we should be though. We should rejoice when the Lord is blessing them and it should be honest not a fake smile and congratulations. The Lord sees right through that, He knows our TRUE thoughts. God may be testing your faithfulness. It is easy to trust Him when everything is going good, not so much when things are falling apart though. My former Preacher, Bro. Steve Parrish always says "A faith that can't be tested, can't be trusted." God may just want you to put ALL your faith in Him so the He can use you to share His word around the world!

TODAY'S TAKE AWAY

(write or doodle your thoughts for the day)

1 SAMUEL 17:29

"And David said, What have I now done? Is there not a cause?"

This is a really familiar verse of scripture where David faces Goliath, most of us have probably heard this story thousands of times and my husband even has a sermon he preaches out of this passage called the types of "Christians you meet." Which is partly where I got the inspiration for this devotional! In his sermon he introduces us to 3 types of Christians which are the Cowardly Christian, the Criticizing Christian, and the Courageous Christian. The one I want to focus on is the Courageous Christian and how we can all become more Courageous!

In the story of David and Goliath, David is just a young boy going into battle to check on his brothers at his father's command. When he arrives he finds his brothers, King Saul and the WHOLE army of Israel scared of one Philistine warrior. Goliath of Gath was his name and he tempted and mocked the name and army of God. Well, when David gets to the scene of the battle and sees what is going on he immediately asks (in paraphrase of course) 'what in the world is going on here! Why is this man defiling God and you all are standing here scared doing nothing?!' David can not believe what he is seeing, but then King Saul gets word that David has come in questioning his tactics he calls for David. When David meets with King Saul, David tells the King that he will go and fight the Philistine. King Saul is very quick to tell David that he would be no match for Goliath, because Goliath has been a man of war for many years, but David doesn't care he just knows that someone is going against God and that's not right. So, King Saul gives David armour and a sword and tells him to go, but David said no, he was not trained with that armour. Instead, he took his staff, his sling, and 5 smooth stones from the brook. Then, David headed towards Goliath, and when Goliath sees him he asked 'who is this youth?' and Goliath mocks David, saying how easy the battle will be and how he will kill David and leave his carcase for the birds. Then,

David informed Goliath that he would be the one that perished that day, because the Lord was on David's side. That's when the battle began Goliath ran towards David, and David drew up his sling and one of the smooth stones and slang it at Goliath hitting him the forehead and killing him on the spot. David then took Goliath's own sword and cut off his head to show the Philistines that Goliath was truly dead. David did it, he defeated Goliath.

I say all of that to say this, David was a very Courageous Christian, and he did not care what it cost him whether that be his family or his life he just wanted to serve God. David knew that what King Saul and the army was doing was wrong and so he did something about it. He stood when no one else would and he showed everyone there that day that if you just put your trust in God he will deliver you. David also didn't let the negativity get to him of everyone telling him that he was just a youth and that he would surely die, he knew God was with him and he had no fear. Lastly, David did not use what other people wanted him to use, he used his staff and sling. He used what God gave him. We could learn alot from David about being a Courageous Christian. He teaches us to be bold, to stand up and to use the gifts that God has given us. So, let's go out and be courageous!

*You can go back and read this whole story in 1 Samuel 17 if you want a more indepth version.

TODAY'S TAKE AWAY
(write or doodle your thoughts for the day)

1 SAMUEL 2:2

"There is none holy as the LORD: for there is none beside thee: neither is there any rock like our God."

Neither is there any rock like our God! This verse truly speaks for itself! WE can come to Him with any burden no matter how big or how small it may seem. He is the rock upon which we stand. "Oh Jesus what a friend is He." That song just fits that verse so well. God is always there for His children He will never leave or forsake us! I can still hear my formers preachers voice in the back of my head saying "If you feel like you're not as close to God as you once were it's because you moved!" That goes back perfectly to this verse because guess what?? ROCKS DON'T MOVE! That's why people use rock, stone and concrete, to build with, because they never move. We serve an immovable God He's the same today, yesterday, and tomorrow. He is the only certainty we have in this world, and if that doesn't make you want to run to Him I don't know what will. He never wavers or forgets He's always been there and He always will be. So, cast your worries and your doubts on Him because He can take it!

TODAY'S TAKE AWAY
(write or doodle your thoughts for the day)

LAMENTATIONS 3: 22-23

Verse 23:
"They are new every morning: great is thy faithfulness."

I woke up this morning with the phrase "every morning His mercies are new" on my mind. So I got online and looked up what verse that was referenced from and it was from Lamentations 3:22-23. In the beginning of this chapter Jeremiah is telling about his sorrows and problems and honestly they seem pretty rough. This goes on for 19 verses, then verse 20 and 21 come in and verse 21 reads "This I recall to my mind, therefore have I hope." (Lamentations, verse 21, chapter 3, KJV) WE HAVE HOPE!! Now, for 22 and 23. God has so much compassion for us. He loves us so much that He gives us a clean slate every day. God always knows just what we need every. single. day. Take my morning for example, my husband and I laid sod yesterday, and by that I mean he laid sod while I sort of helped. When you lay new sod you have to water it so that it doesn't wither and die. Wouldn't you know it this morning we woke up to to rain! He watered our sod for us! Now, you may not, but I count that as a gift from God. If He cares enough about us to meet a need as meaningless as watering grass, just think about what He could do with the real needs in your life. Every morning His grace and mercies are new that means He NEVER runs out! No matter how many times we come to Him, He is always right there.

TODAY'S TAKE AWAY
(write or doodle your thoughts for the day)

MATTHEW 6:21

"For where your treasure is, there will your heart be also."

Starting in verse 19 of chapter 6 Jesus is teaching us about money, and having treasures down here on Earth. He tells us not to put all of our treasures down here, but to instead put them in Heaven because worldly treasures will fade away. That new house, it'll become old and crumble. That new car, it will depreciate as soon as you get it off of the lot. We shouldn't put our trust in these worldly things because they will eventually become old and worn out. But, Jesus says that if we put or treasures in Heaven that they will never get old or worn out! My house down here may not be new, but my mansion up in Heaven is sparkling new never to grow old! My former preacher Bro. Steve Parrish always says "There's nothing wrong with having stuff, as long as your stuff doesn't have you." That is so true, we are so prone to get wrapped up in wanting to have the newest, or the best, or even the most, and we shouldn't be like that! This brings me to verse 21 "For where your treasure is, there will be your heart also." (Matthew, verse 21, chapter 6, KJV) Sadly, how true this is. If our heart is on the things of this world then that means it's not on God. You can only have one God. If that "god" is the world then you aren't doing for the cause of Christ, you've lost your salt for God. But, if the God of the universe is the God you serve then your treasures may not be the best, biggest, or newest on Earth but they will be in Heaven.

TODAY'S TAKE AWAY
(write or doodle your thoughts for the day)

GENESIS 22

"And Abraham said, My son, God will provide himself a lamb for a burnt offering: so they went both of them together."

Whenever I think of the story of Abraham and Isaac I always think of the song "When I lay my Isaac down", that song is about laying down the most important thing in our lives because God tells us to. I, personally, don't have any children right now, but I could not imagine killing my own child. In Genesis 22 it starts out with God telling Abraham to take Isaac and make him a burnt offering. That had to have been the saddest thing Abraham has ever heard God say. If you know anything about about the story of Abraham his wife Sarah and he were too old to have children. Abraham was 100 when Isaac was born so you could call him a miracle baby in today's terms. Abraham loved Isaac, he was his ONLY son. God just told Abraham to kill him, but instead of telling God no or running from God, Abraham got up the next morning saddled his donkeys and set out for the mountain with Isaac. Once they got close Isaac asked where the lamb for the offering was, to which Abraham replies "My son, God will provide himself a lamb for a burnt offering..."(Genesis, verse 8, chapter 22, KJV). So they made it to the mountain and Abraham sets up the altar and then the bible says Abraham bound Isaac. So between verse 8 an 9 Abraham had to have told Isaac that he's the offering. I could not in my wildest dreams imagine the emotion that is going though both of them at that time. Then, there is verse 10 "And Abraham stretched for his hand and took the knife to slay his son." (Mathew, verse 10, chapter 22, KJV) Abraham had the knife in his hand so willing to follow God and the plan He had for his life. Then, and angel called down from heaven and told him (in our words) Don't do it! The angel tells Abraham that he has shown himself and that he truly fears God because he held nothing back from God, not even his son. When Abraham looked up he seen a ram caught in a bush, isn't that just like God, always having exactly what we need just at the right time. So the ram took

Isaac's place just like Jesus took our place on the cross. If that isn't love, I don't know what is. Abraham was so sold out to God that even though what God asked him to do is what hurt him the most he still did it, because he knew that God's plan is greater than any plan he could have for his own life. While, I highly doubt God would now ask us to sacrifice our children in that specific manner, are you sacrificing the things God is asking for you to sacrifice so you can spend time with him in his word, maybe there are some people in your life you know you don't need to be hanging out with, or maybe some places you shouldn't be going. Are you heeding to what God is telling you? Are you laying your Isaac down? There's no telling what God has planned for you, He's just waiting on you to get some things out of the way.

TODAY'S TAKE AWAY
(write or doodle your thoughts for the day)

PHILIPPIANS 3:13-14

Verse 14:
*"I press toward the mark for the prize of the high
calling of God in Christ Jesus"*

On my mail route I stop at a small gas station in Troy. While I was there Saturday the owner and I were talking about how much mail we had that day and that the trucks had run late. We talked for a few minutes more and then he smiled and said "Hey, the best you can do, is the best you can do." That phrase stuck with me all that day and all that weekend. What is the best that we, as Christians, can do? So, I went home and searched on google about all the different times the Bible mentions doing your best, and the verses in Philippians popped up and I just knew that was what God wanted me to see.

So many times I feel like we can't do our best for God because we are stuck on our past failures and shortcomings keeping us from focusing on what God wants us to do in the now. The devil will bring up those specific failures to keep you in fear of what God is wanting you to do, because honestly who reallllly likes to fail, no one! And, the devil will use that against us big time, but in the second part of verse 13 it goes on to say "Forgetting those things which are behind, and reaching forth unto those things which are before" (Philippians, verse 13, chapter 3, KJV) If you are a forgiven blood bought child of God then our yesterdays are already forgiven! God has "forgotten" them so why can't we! WE can't let our past sins keep us from our future works. Think about if Thomas Edison would have given up on the lightbulb after about that 500th failure, we wouldn't have the light technology that we have today, but guess what?! He didn't let his past failures define him. He just kept looking at all the possibilities ahead and kept trying until he succeeded, that's how we should be! Every day we must press towards the mark for God. Even if that means just doing something as simple as speaking a kind word to a stranger. If that's the best we can do, then that is our best! Let me leave you with one question.

Are you doing your best?

ABOUT THE AUTHOR

Karye Lynn McCord is a 21 year old, wife, youth leader, co-owner of www. thepositiveforchrist.com with a dear friend Hayden Jenkins, and dog mom! She was saved at the age of 18 at a tent revival in Hurricane Mississippi. She has always loved to write, which brought forth The Positive For Christ. She wanted a positive space to share Christ in her life and what Christ is doing in the lives of others. This book in her newest endeavor to share  the Gospel to the world in a manner that relatable to the people around her. She hopes to help people who are struggling with the "perfect" image that the world has of a Christian woman. She sees the pressure that is put on young women and how people love to bring out the failures and mess ups. Karye has written a book of 30 devotionals to help the girl who feels less than perfect in a world of "perfection". She hopes to help and encourage her fellow Christians.

NOTES

NOTES

NOTES

NOTES

NOTES

NOTES

NOTES

NOTES

NOTES

NOTES

NOTES

NOTES

NOTES

NOTES

NOTES

NOTES

NOTES

_____

_____

_____

_____

_____

_____

_____

_____

_____

_____

_____

_____

_____

_____

_____

NOTES

NOTES

NOTES

NOTES

NOTES

NOTES

NOTES

NOTES

NOTES

NOTES

NOTES

NOTES

NOTES

NOTES

Printed in the United States
By Bookmasters